Amelia Earhart

History Maker Bios

Jane Sutcliffe

Green Garden
Library

⌐ LERNER PUBLICATIONS COMPANY • MINNEAPOLIS

For Meghan, Garrett, Erin, Luke, and Noah

Map on p. 45 by Laura Westlund
Illustrations by Tim Parlin

Text copyright © 2003 by Jane Sutcliffe
Illustrations copyright © 2003 by Lerner Publications Company

Lerner Publications Company
A division of Lerner Publishing Group
241 First Avenue North
Minneapolis, MN 55401 U.S.A.

Website address: www.lernerbooks.com

Library of Congress Cataloging-in-Publication Data

Sutcliffe, Jane.
    Amelia Earhart / by Jane Sutcliffe.
        p.   cm. — (History maker bios)
    Summary: Traces the life of the famous pilot, focusing on her record setting
flights in the 1920s and 1930s and her inspiration to other women.
    Includes bibliographical references and index.
    ISBN: 0–8225–0396–4 (lib. bdg. : alk. paper)
    1. Earhart, Amelia, 1897–1937—Juvenile literature. 2. Women air pilots—
United States—Biography—Juvenile literature. 3. Air pilots—United States—
Biography—Juvenile literature. [1. Earhart, Amelia, 1897–1937. 2. Air pilots.
3. Women—Biography.] I. Title. II. Series.
TL540.E3 S88   2003
629.13'092—dc21   2002000945

Manufactured in the United States of America
1 2 3 4 5 6 – JR – 08 07 06 05 04 03

TABLE OF CONTENTS

INTRODUCTION

Amelia Earhart was one of the most famous pilots in the world. She became a pilot in the days when flying was new. Amelia was a daring flier. She flew across oceans and continents. She set record after record. Many of her flights were firsts, not just for a female pilot, but for any pilot.

Amelia followed her dreams. She showed people that women can and should do anything men do. Because of her, many young women dare to follow their own dreams.

This is her story.

1 "JUST LIKE FLYING!"

Amelia Earhart was born on July 24, 1897, in Atchison, Kansas. When Amelia was growing up, little girls were supposed to behave like young ladies. But Amelia didn't.

Young ladies didn't jump over fences, her grandmother scolded. But Amelia did.

Young ladies wore dresses with ruffled aprons. But Amelia didn't. She wore loose pants called bloomers when she went out to play. She said they made her feel free and athletic.

Amelia's grandmother shook her head at Amelia's tomboy ways. Her parents, though, didn't worry about what was proper. They gave baseballs and footballs to Amelia and her sister, Muriel. Mr. Earhart played cowboys-and-Indians with his girls.

Amelia (LEFT) and Muriel were supposed to act like young ladies, according to their grandmother.

Amelia liked all kinds of sports and games. She liked taking risks, too. Once she saw a roller coaster at a fair. Her mother said the wobbly thing was too dangerous to ride. So Amelia made her own roller coaster. She nailed boards to the side of the tool shed. A crate with wheels was the car. When she finished, she got in and zoomed down the track. "It's just like flying!" she told her sister.

Wearing bloomers, Muriel swings and Amelia walks on stilts.

At another
fair, Amelia
saw an airplane
for the first time.

In 1903, the Wright Brothers made the first airplane flight.

The Wright brothers had flown the first plane just five years before. Most people thought the new machines were exciting. Amelia didn't. She called it "a thing of rusty wire and wood." She didn't give it another thought.

Amelia graduated from high school in 1915. She was tall and slim. She had a shy smile that showed a little gap between her front teeth. Her calm gray eyes looked right at you when she spoke.

After high school, Amelia went to the Ogontz School in Pennsylvania. For Christmas vacation in 1917, Amelia visited her sister. Muriel was a student in Toronto, Canada. Canadian soldiers had been fighting in World War I for a few years. For the first time, Amelia saw injured soldiers. Some were blind. Others had no arms or legs.

Amelia wanted to do something to help. She decided to quit school and become a nurse's aide in Canada.

She worked ten-hour days in a military hospital. She scrubbed floors and carried trays. She tried to cheer up the sick and wounded men.

She made time for fun, too. One time Amelia and another girl went to an air show. Pilots were performing stunts in their airplanes. One pilot dove his plane straight at the two girls as a joke. Amelia's friend ran off, frightened. Amelia didn't. She was fascinated. "That little red airplane said something to me as it swished by," she said.

Amelia was a nurse's aide in Canada in 1918.

In 1918 the war ended. Amelia decided she wanted to study medicine. She became a student at Columbia University in New York. For a year, Amelia studied hard and did well. Then she received a letter from her parents. They had moved to Los Angeles, California. They wanted her to come, too. Amelia agreed—but just for the summer. "After that I'm going to come back here and live my own life," she wrote to her sister.

When she was in California, Amelia went to an air show. A few days later, she paid one dollar for her first airplane ride. As soon as Amelia left the ground, she knew she had to learn to fly.

2 AMELIA IN THE AIR

I want to fly. Can you teach me?"
Amelia had come to an airfield in Los
Angeles to see Neta Snook. Neta was a
pilot and a flying instructor. She agreed to
teach Amelia to fly.

Amelia learned fast. Neta called her a
"natural."

Neta Snook (LEFT) taught Amelia how to fly at Kinner Airfield.

Sometimes, though, Amelia earned a scolding from Neta. There were two high-tension wires at the end of the airfield's runway. Pilots were supposed to fly above the wires. Amelia liked to fly *between* them—even though the wires were only eight feet apart!

Amelia loved being up in the sky. But she could only fly on weekends. She had a job at the phone company to pay for her lessons. "No pay, no fly, and no work, no pay," she liked to say.

That summer, for her twenty-fourth birthday, Amelia got the best present she could imagine: her own plane. Her mother and sister put their money together to buy it for her. Soon Amelia was not just going to air shows. She was flying in them. In one air show, she flew her plane higher than any woman had before.

Amelia seemed to have everything she wanted. She had a job. She had her own plane. She even had a boyfriend. His name was Sam Chapman.

Amelia's mother loved this photo of Amelia in her flying gear.

In 1924, when Amelia was twenty-seven, Mr. and Mrs. Earhart divorced. Muriel was teaching in Massachusetts, and Mrs. Earhart wanted to join her. She wanted Amelia to come, too. So Amelia sold her plane and bought a car. She and her mother drove across the country to Medford, Massachusetts.

Sam Chapman followed Amelia east. He wanted to marry her. But Sam didn't want a wife with a job. Amelia dreamed of a career. She said a married woman in the 1920s lived the life of a "robot." That kind of life was not for her.

Amelia (LEFT) and Sam Chapman had fun together, swimming and playing tennis.

Amelia got a job as a social worker in nearby Boston. She worked at a community center for new immigrants. Amelia taught English to adults. She helped set up games and plays for children. On weekends she went flying in borrowed planes.

One day in April 1928, Amelia received a phone call at the center. The caller was Captain Hilton Railey. He had an amazing question: "Would you fly the Atlantic?"

Charles Lindbergh flew the SPIRIT OF ST. LOUIS solo from New York to Paris in 1927.

Charles Lindbergh had made his famous solo flight across the Atlantic Ocean the year before. But no woman had ever crossed the Atlantic—not even as a passenger. If Amelia made it, she would be the first!

Captain Railey explained that a seaplane called the *Friendship* was ready to fly from North America to Europe. Two male pilots, Bill Stultz and Slim Gordon, would fly the plane. Another woman had planned to go along. But her family would not let her make such a dangerous trip. Would Amelia go in her place?

Amelia hesitated for only a second. Then she said yes.

To make the long trip, extra gas tanks were crowded into the seaplane's cabin. There was barely room for Amelia. Her only luggage was a toothbrush, a comb, and an extra scarf. On June 17, 1928, the *Friendship* left Newfoundland, Canada.

The FRIENDSHIP takes off.

Forecasts had called for clear weather. But the *Friendship* was surrounded by clouds. Then the radio stopped working. The crew had planned to contact ships to find out where they were. Now there was no way to do that. And they couldn't see much through the heavy clouds and fog.

Suddenly, there was a break in the clouds. The crew spotted a ship.

Amelia peeks out from the FRIENDSHIP after landing in Wales.

Amelia wrote a note. She asked the ship's captain to paint its position on the deck of the ship. That way the *Friendship's* crew could see where they were, too. She put the note in a bag. She added two oranges for weight and dropped the bag. She missed. The bag—note, fruit, and all— just splashed into the ocean.

At last Bill Stultz spotted some fishing boats. Then they saw it—land! They put the plane down in a small harbor. But they still weren't sure where they were.

A man rowed a boat out to the *Friendship.* "We've come from America," Amelia told him.

"Have ye now?" the man said. "Well, I'm sure we wish you welcome to Burry Port, Wales."

3 FLIGHT PLANS

Suddenly Amelia was famous. Everyone asked her how it felt to be the first woman to fly across the Atlantic. Amelia was surprised at the attention. She told them she felt like a "sack of potatoes." The men had done the flying, she said. "I was just baggage."

The three fliers sailed back to the United States. Parades were held all over the country in their honor. Wherever they went, people jostled each other for a glimpse of Amelia. Publisher George Palmer Putnam asked her to write a book about the flight. Amelia's book was called *20 Hrs. 40 Min.*— the length of her flight.

Putnam realized that people would pay to see Amelia. He helped schedule lectures for her. Amelia spoke to women's clubs and business groups about flying.

English children cheer Amelia after the FRIENDSHIP flight. She called herself "a social worker who flies for sport."

More and more, Amelia began to depend on G. P. Putnam. He arranged her schedules and gave her advice. One day, he asked Amelia to marry him. Amelia still wasn't sure about marriage. She said no. But G. P. *was* sure. He asked her again— and again—and again. In all, G. P. asked Amelia six times. The last time, Amelia nodded her head yes. On February 7, 1931, the two were married.

Amelia Earhart and George Palmer Putnam

Amelia used the money she earned from her book to buy a new plane, a Lockheed Vega.

At breakfast one day, Amelia looked up from her newspaper. "Would you mind if I flew the Atlantic?" she asked her husband.

Of course, it didn't matter if G. P. minded or not. Amelia was going. This time, she'd be more than "just baggage." This time, she'd be the pilot—the only pilot. She was going to fly the Atlantic solo.

By April 1932, Amelia and her plane were ready. But bad weather kept her on the ground. At last Amelia was able to fly to Newfoundland to begin her flight.

Amelia climbs into the cockpit of her Lockheed Vega.

On the evening of May 20, 1932, Amelia climbed into her cockpit. Then she headed out to sea. The date made Amelia happy. It marked exactly five years since Charles Lindbergh had flown across the Atlantic.

At first the weather was fair. Amelia watched the moon rise over some clouds. Then she flew into a storm. Lightning flashed around her. Winds shook her plane. Amelia flew higher to get above the storm. The higher she went, the colder the air became. Ice formed on the plane's wings. The ice made the plane heavy and slow.

Amelia brought the plane lower to melt the ice in the warmer air. Suddenly, she saw waves breaking just beneath her. She was too low! Back up she went. All night, Amelia tried to keep her plane in the middle—not too high or too low.

A few hours later, Amelia looked out a window. There were flames coming from the engine! She knew that the damage would only get worse. But there was nothing to do but go on.

By morning, Amelia's plane was shaking badly. Amelia needed to land—now. She spotted the coast of Ireland passing beneath her. She circled above a pasture, "frightening all the cattle in the county."

NATIONAL TREASURES

The red Lockheed Vega airplane that Amelia flew on her solo Atlantic flight is on display at the National Air and Space Museum in Washington, D.C. The leather jacket and goggles she wore that night are there, too.

Amelia landed her plane just outside Londonderry, Ireland. As the plane's wheels touched the ground, Amelia made history. She was the first woman to fly across the Atlantic alone. And she was the first person ever to make the flight twice.

Amelia is cheered by crowds after her arrival in Ireland.

4 A Taste For Records

Amelia was not just a famous "sack of potatoes" anymore. President Herbert Hoover awarded her the gold medal of the National Geographic Society. Scientists and government officials came to watch the award ceremony. Thousands of people listened on the radio.

New York City gives Amelia a ticker-tape parade.

Amelia thought everyone was making too big a fuss. She said that she just hoped "the flight has meant something to women in aviation."

Amelia still earned money by speaking about her flights. She traveled all over the country giving speeches. But she also wanted to break more records. She needed the adventure of doing something new. That was just fine with Amelia's fans. The more records Amelia broke, the more people wanted to see her.

Some pilots set records by flying faster than anyone else. Some flew higher. Amelia flew farther. Most pilots got sleepy on long flights. Not Amelia. Her energy helped her tackle new long-distance records.

Only a few months after her Atlantic flight, Amelia flew nonstop across the United States, from California to New Jersey. It took her a little over nineteen hours. It was a new women's record.

A SPECIAL RIDE

In 1933 Franklin D. Roosevelt became president. The Roosevelts invited Amelia to the White House often. The first lady, Eleanor Roosevelt, became a good friend. One night, at a formal dinner, Eleanor told Amelia that she had never been flying at night. So Amelia borrowed a plane. She and Eleanor—still in gowns and gloves—went for a ride under the stars.

A year later, she broke her own record. This time she finished the flight in just over seventeen hours. In the early days of flying, the idea of crossing the continent in under a day was thrilling. Amelia's flights were big news.

Amelia knew that flying over land was one thing. There was always someplace to put the plane down in an emergency. It was much riskier to fly over water. Amelia set her sights on the Pacific Ocean. In January 1935, she became the first person—man or woman—to fly solo across the Pacific Ocean. She flew from Hawaii to California.

Amelia is welcomed in Hawaii.

*Amelia lands in California after flying from Hawaii. That
spring she also became the first person to fly solo from
California to Mexico City.*

Amelia liked to call her flights "hops."
Her next flight would be much more than a
hop. In a series of hops, Amelia planned to
fly around the world. Other pilots had made
round-the-world flights. But Amelia
planned to do it at the equator. That was
the longest route—27,000 miles. No one
had ever done that before.

Other pilots told her the trip was too
dangerous. They wanted her to change her
mind. But Amelia wouldn't. Even if she
crashed, she said, "it will be doing the
thing I've always wanted to do."

Amelia stands in the cockpit of her Lockheed Electra, looking over blueprints.

It took Amelia almost a year to get ready. She needed a bigger, more modern airplane. Amelia chose a Lockheed Electra. The Electra was huge—fifty-five feet from wingtip to wingtip. It had two engines and could fly up to four thousand miles without refueling. The plane was ready on July 24, 1936. It was Amelia's thirty-ninth birthday.

Amelia would not be making her trip alone. A navigator would be going along. He would keep the plane on course. Amelia would do the flying.

The navigator's hardest job would be crossing the Pacific Ocean. The Electra could not carry enough fuel to fly all the way across the Pacific. Amelia planned to stop at Howland Island for fuel. But Howland was only two miles long and a half-mile wide. The navigator would have to find the tiny island in the great ocean.

G. P. says good-bye to Amelia before she leaves on her round-the-world flight.

On March 17, 1937, Amelia began her round-the-world flight. But it was a false start. Only three days later, she damaged the Electra on a bad takeoff. It would take months to repair the plane. But it didn't matter. Amelia wouldn't let anything keep her from making her flight around the world.

The Electra takes off on the first leg of Amelia's round-the-world flight.

3 AROUND THE WORLD

At dawn on June 1, 1937, Amelia took off from Miami, Florida. Her navigator was Fred Noonan. It would take Amelia and Fred a few days to reach the equator. The idea was to fly a circle around the earth. At the end of the trip, they would land right back in the United States. Amelia called it going to California "by about the longest route we could contrive."

Fred (LEFT) and Amelia (CENTER) eat lunch during a stop in Venezuela.

The first stop was Puerto Rico. From there Amelia flew to South America. Then she crossed the Atlantic to Africa. Over the next week, she "hopped" her way across the African continent. By the time they reached India, Amelia and Fred had been traveling for two weeks. They were halfway around the world.

Most days, Amelia was up by three or four in the morning. That way, she and Fred could take off by sunup. They flew on to stops across Southeast Asia. On June 28, Amelia and Fred landed in Australia. The next day, they were in New Guinea. It was their last stop before crossing the wide Pacific. They had covered 22,000 miles. There were only two more stops to make. The first was Howland Island. It was 2,556 miles away.

AMELIA CROSSES THE EQUATOR—DRY!
Fred Noonan had crossed the equator before. But it was Amelia's first time. According to tradition, sailors crossing the equator for the first time get doused with water by their shipmates. So Fred brought along a thermos of water. He planned to dump it on Amelia when the time came. But when they crossed the equator, they were busy. Fred forgot to give Amelia her soaking!

AMELIA'S EQUATOR DUNKING

A coast guard ship, the *Itasca*, was anchored near Howland Island. The *Itasca* would help guide Amelia and Fred to the tiny dot in the Pacific. The crew was standing by to radio Amelia. The ship would also send up a plume of black smoke as a signal.

On July 2, Amelia took off from New Guinea. She flew for more than fourteen hours. Finally the *Itasca* crew heard her voice. But it wasn't clear. No one could understand what she was saying.

Amelia and Fred check a map that shows the route of their flight to Howland Island.

The ITASCA, anchored off Howland Island, listened for Amelia and Fred.

An hour later, they heard her again. The radio operator on the *Itasca* asked, "What is your position? When do you expect to reach Howland?" There was no answer.

On and off over the next few hours, the *Itasca* crew heard Amelia's voice. Sometimes there was so much static they could barely understand her. Sometimes she asked them to "take a bearing" on her. She was asking for her position. But she could not hear their messages. It was clear she was lost.

Amelia adjusts the radio in the Electra.

By this time, Amelia had been flying for nineteen hours. She was more than an hour overdue. Then the *Itasca* heard her say: "We must be on you but cannot see you but gas is running low. Been unable to reach you by radio." Minutes later came another message: "We are circling but cannot hear you."

Over and over, the *Itasca* tried to reach Amelia. The crew knew that she was running out of fuel. She must also be exhausted. They could only wait and watch the sky.

An hour later, they heard Amelia's voice again. " . . . We are running north and south," she said. Then there was silence. Amelia and Fred had simply vanished.

For two weeks, thousands of rescuers searched for Amelia's plane. They found nothing. Amelia never came home.

Amelia Earhart was one of the most famous women in the world when she vanished. Her disappearance shocked people everywhere.

We may never know how Amelia died. But we do know how she lived. She was a person of daring and determination. Amelia did not finish her last flight. But she would have been disappointed if she had not tried.

TIMELINE

AMELIA EARHART
WAS BORN ON
JULY 24, 1897.

In the year . . .

1903   the Wright brothers flew the first airplane.

1915   Amelia graduated from Hyde Park High School in Chicago.   Age 17

1917   she became a nurse's aide in Toronto, Canada.

1921   she took flying lessons from Neta Snook. she got her first airplane in July.   Age 24

1922   she set her first record, flying to a height of 14,000 feet.

1927   Charles Lindbergh became the first person to fly solo across the Atlantic Ocean.

1928   she became the first woman to fly across the Atlantic, as a passenger on the *Friendship.*   Age 30

1931   she married George Palmer Putnam.   Age 33

1932   she became the first woman to fly solo across the Atlantic and the first person to cross the Atlantic twice by air in May. she set a women's record for the fastest flight across the United States in August.   Age 34

1935   she became the first person to fly solo across the Pacific Ocean, from Honolulu, Hawaii, to Oakland, California, in January. she was the first person to fly solo from Los Angeles, California, to Mexico City, Mexico, in April.

1936   she began her round-the-world flight with navigator Fred Noonan in June.

1937   she disappeared near Howland Island in the Pacific on July 2.   Age 39

WHAT HAPPENED TO AMELIA?

People have come up with many ideas to explain Amelia's disappearance. Some wondered if Amelia and Fred landed on a deserted island. From time to time, people have found bits of wreckage, bones, and even shoes on such islands. Perhaps these belonged to Amelia or Fred.

Others thought that the Japanese government captured Amelia and Fred. Amelia's last flight took place a few years before World War II. The United States and Japan were not on friendly terms. If Amelia and Fred had been found by the Japanese, they might have been killed as spies. Some people even wondered if Amelia and Fred really were spying for the U.S. government.

No one has ever found anything to prove these stories. Most people believe that Amelia's plane simply ran out of gas and crashed into the Pacific Ocean.

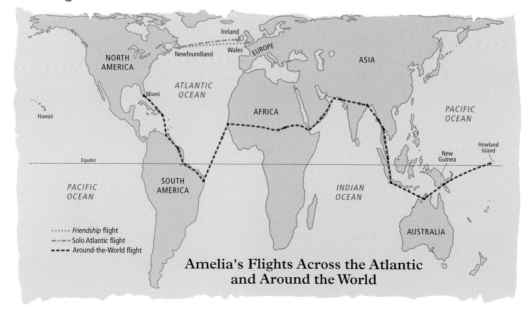

Amelia's Flights Across the Atlantic and Around the World

FURTHER READING

Bowen, Andy Russell. *Flying against the Wind: A Story about Beryl Markham.* **Minneapolis: Carolrhoda Books, 1998.** The life of the aviator who was raised in Kenya and made the first flight from east to west across the Atlantic.

Cummins, Julie. *Tomboy of the Air: Daredevil Pilot Blanche Stuart Scott.* **New York: HarperCollins, 2001.** The life of the first American woman to fly an airplane.

Lindbergh, Reeve. *Nobody Owns the Sky: The Story of "Brave Bessie" Coleman.* **Cambridge, MA: Candlewick Press, 1996.** A picture book biography of the first African American to have a pilot's license.

Ryan, Pam Muñoz. *Amelia and Eleanor Go for a Ride.* **New York: Scholastic, 1999.** A picture book about the night Amelia Earhart and Eleanor Roosevelt left a White House party and went flying.

Zaunders, Bo. *Feathers, Flaps, and Flops: Fabulous Early Fliers.* **New York: Dutton, 2001.** The stories of some lesser-known early fliers, including the Montgolfier brothers, Jimmy Doolittle, and "Wrong Way" Corrigan.

WEBSITES

Amelia Earhart Birthplace Museum
<http://www.ameliaearhartmuseum.org/>
A tour of Amelia's house in Atchison, Kansas.

The Ninety-Nines (Amelia Earhart page)
<http://www.ninety-nines.org/earhart.html>
A timeline of Amelia's life on the International Organization of Women Pilots website. Explore the entire site.

SELECT BIBLIOGRAPHY

"Amelia Earhart to Circle Globe in Her 'Flying Laboratory' Plane." *New York Times,* 12 February 1937, p. 25.

Butler, Susan. *East to the Dawn: The Life of Amelia Earhart.* Reading, MA: Addison-Wesley, 1997.

Earhart, Amelia. *The Fun of It: Random Records of My Own Flying and of Women in Aviation.* New York: Brewer, Warren, & Putnam, 1932.

Earhart, Amelia. *Last Flight.* New York: Harcourt, 1937.

Earhart, Amelia. *Letters from Amelia, 1901–1937.* Edited by Jean L. Backus. Boston: Beacon Press, 1982.

Earhart, Amelia. *20 Hrs. 40 Min.: Our Flight in the Friendship.* New York: Putnam, 1928.

Lovell, Mary S. *The Sound of Wings: The Life of Amelia Earhart.* New York: St. Martin's Press, 1989.

"Miss Earhart Forced Down at Sea, Howland Island Fears; Coast Guard Begins Search." *New York Times,* 3 July 1937, p. 1.

Morrissey, Muriel Earhart. *Courage Is the Price: The Life of Amelia Earhart.* Wichita, KS: McCormick-Armstrong, 1963.

Putnam, George Palmer. *Soaring Wings: A Biography of Amelia Earhart.* New York: Harcourt, 1939.

Spencer, Alex, Curator in Aeronautics, National Air and Space Museum. Interview by the author, 6 November 2001.

INDEX

Acknowledgments

For photographs and artwork: © Bettmann/Corbis, pp. 4, 16, 19, 30, 32, 34, 35, 36, 38, 40, 41; The Arthur and Elizabeth Schlesinger Library, pp. 7, 8; Smithsonian National Air and Space Museum, pp. 9, 18, 25, 33, 42; Harcourt, Brace, p. 11; Purdue University Libraries Special Collections, p. 14; © Topical Press Agency/ Archive Photos, pp. 15, 20, 23, 26; © Archive Photos, p. 24; © Keystone/Archive Photos, p. 28. Front cover: © Archive Photos. Back cover: Smithsonian National Postal Museum.

For quoted material: pp. 8, 12, 16, 22, Muriel Earhart Morrissey, *Courage Is the Price: The Life of Amelia Earhart* (Wichita, KS: McCormick-Armstrong, 1963); pp. 9, 11, 37, Amelia Earhart, *Last Flight* (New York: Harcourt, Brace, 1937); p. 13, Susan Butler, *East to the Dawn: The Life of Amelia Earhart* (Reading, MA: Addison-Wesley, 1997); pp. 14, 17, 27, Amelia Earhart, *The Fun of It: Random Records of My Own Flying and of Women in Aviation* (New York: Brewer, Warren, & Putnam, 1932); pp. 10, 22, 23, Doris Rich, *Amelia Earhart: A Biography* (Washington, D.C.: Smithsonian University Press, 1989); pp. 21, 25, George Palmer Putnam, *Soaring Wings: a Biography of Amelia Earhart* (New York: Harcourt, 1939); p. 30, Amelia Earhart, *Letters from Amelia, 1901–1937,* ed. Jean L. Backus (Boston: Beacon Press, 1982); p. 33, Nancy Shore, *Amelia Earhart* (New York: Chelsea House, 1987); pp. 41–43, Mary S. Lovell, *The Sound of Wings: The Life of Amelia Earhart* (New York: St. Martin's Press, 1989).